Leadership

The Keys to Becoming a

Person of Influence in

Business & in Life

Steve Gold

Table of Contents

owner. All trademarks and brands within this book are for clarifying purposes only and are the owned by the owners themselves, not affiliated with this document.

<u>Introduction</u>

It is commonly assumed – especially in the cut-throat corporate world – that being a leader is a prestigious position. It certainly comes with some perks; authority over others, a salary raise, additional benefits in the organization and perhaps a corner office. Ascending to a leadership position at work can certainly be considered some sort of career milestone and achievement.

In actual fact, it is rather misleading to equate the outer indicators of leadership with success. Leadership is so much more than the title and the privileges that come with it. Having to lead others is a position of great responsibility, and it takes certain personality traits for a person to become, not only a competent, but also an effective and thus well-respected leader.

As you are about to learn, great leadership is not simply a mythical personality trait that some people seem to be born with. Leadership is a skill that can be learned and honed. There are factors that could play a part in making certain people better leaders than others, but essentially anyone can train themselves to be a better leader.

In this book, you will be guided through the steps you can take in order to be a better leader by taking action to make improvements in various aspects of your personality, character and mindset. You will find out what it actually means to be a great leader, the habits you can cultivate to better lead both yourself and others, and the thought patterns that may be currently holding you back. Above all, you will work on building greater self-confidence, which is the foundation to effective leadership.

Although most of the guidance offered here is geared towards improving your effectiveness in leading in a work setting, you will find these skills to be applicable in both your personal and professional live.

Chapter 1

Defining Leadership

A very straight forward basic definition of a leader is a person with followers. Being a leader certainly puts you in a position to tell others what to do, but there is a big difference between an effective leader who is respected by his or her followers, and a leader only by title. Before you can learn to become a good leader, let's start by understanding what constitutes good leadership.

Being a Leader vs. Being a Boss

Although we often associate leadership with being a boss, the notion could never be further from the truth. Bosses are simply people who have authority over a team of workers under his or her charge, while leaders aspire to bring out the best in their followers. Consider the following comparison of leaders and bosses:

Leader	Boss
• Develop and empower others to excel	• Instruct others to complete tasks
• Motivate others to be their best	• Set rules and instructions for those under their charge to follow
• Acknowledge and celebrate success as a team effort	• Takes credit for the team's achievements
• Make plans driven by a vision for excellence	• Make plans to get a job done
• Respected, liked and valued by followers	• Obeyed (at times feared and resented) by followers
• People work with the leader	• People work for the boss

Redefining What it Means to Lead

Because leadership is commonly associated with wielding authority, qualities such as intelligence, adaptability, and assertiveness usually come to mind as being important to developing leadership skills. While there is some truth to this, such a perception of competent leadership is limiting and outdated.

Attitudes in the working world are changing, with companies becoming less structured and traditional job roles becoming more obscure. As such, the conventional superior-subordinate dynamic is increasingly seen as rigid, inefficient and ineffective. This calls for a departure from authoritative corporate leadership in favor of a more egalitarian and transformative style. Various studies by leading business publications have shown that companies that strive to inspire, encourage and develop employees tend to have a higher performing workforce.

In summation, leading effectively means to empower others to grow and surpass their personal bests. To do that, one needs to first bypass the outer indicators of being a leader, and give more focus to personal development of the individual.

Chapter 2

Habits of Highly Effective Leaders

Great leaders are made, not born. In fact, effective leadership stems from the accumulation of good personal habits that foster certain qualities in an individual, enabling them to inspire and guide others to greater heights. In essence, anyone can learn to become a competent leader. It starts with a conscious decision to cultivate certain ways of thinking and doing things, which are then practiced until they become automated behaviors.

It Starts with You!

Before you have the capacity to competently lead others, you have to first be your own leader and take charge of your own life. As an example, let's look at the story of Carl the window cleaner:

50 year-old Carl is one of the custodians at a commercial building that housed some of the most prestigious law, tech and business firms in town. For more than a decade since he was employed, he has shown a consistent record of showing for work on-time almost every morning – save for the occasional family emergency and medical leave. Because he shows no fear for heights, he has been tasked to clean the large glass windows of the 20th floor. Every day,

like clockwork, Carl would clean the same windows three times; in the morning, after lunch and before heading home. He ensures the windows are spotless, because it is his job. He does this with an understanding of how important it is for the businesses that operate in the building to project a classy image to visitors. Carl's cleaning routine is so ingrained that he does not even have to think about it. Throughout the years, his work ethic has caught the attention of other custodians that then began emulating him.

Carl's story demonstrates what it is like to be one's own leader. He does not have a team of staff answering to him, neither is his job a glamorous one. However, Carl understands that he has a role to fulfill and a purpose to serve – as small as that purpose may be in the grand scheme of things. Hence, he took it upon himself to give it his very best every day on the job, leading by example and inspiring others to follow suit. Carl is therefore a leader.

The moral of the story is that regardless of your position on the corporate ladder – or where you are in life, for that matter – leadership skills will always serve you well.

The Personal Leadership Action Plan

By now, you should already have a basic idea of the qualities that account for good leadership. The key is to remember that becoming an effective leader is a choice, but it does involve action on one's part to cultivate the required habits and mindset.

Here is a blueprint of what you want to incorporate into your daily life when aspiring to be a better leader. Be sure to follow the simple thought exercises along the way. Spend some time to think about them, and consider jotting down your thoughts so as to make them more concrete. Also, feel free to revisit any of the points here later on, if needed.

1. Believe in and be passionate about what you do.

Effective leaders inspire others to follow along because they have a genuine passion and enthusiasm for what it is that they do. Their passion comes from the belief that they are adding value to the lives of others. If you feel that your job is insignificant and you are easily replaceable, it would help to adopt a "bigger picture outlook" and recognize that you have a service to offer.

Exercise

Consider your current job role and responsibilities. How does your job performance affect the organization's daily operations as a whole? If your job were to be removed, how would that impact the people (clients and customers) that the company serves?

2. Define your core values and live by them.

Have you ever made choices only for your decisions to have lead to a nagging feeling of unease you just couldn't shake off? You likely felt this way because you knew at the back of your mind that the decisions you made were against your core values and what you truly believed to be right.

When one's actions are at odds with their ethics, our subconscious becomes occupied with feelings of guilt and caution, hindering thoughts that are conducive to productivity and success in any endeavor. However, when our thoughts and actions are aligned with our personal values and ethics, our conscience remains clear. In addition, we will garner more trust from people when they sense integrity in our words and actions.

Exercise

Think back to a time where you made a decision or do something which you were not proud of, only for it to have haunted your conscience. Examine why it made you feel bad. Was it because you went against your personal code of ethics? Was someone or something compromised along the way? What would you have don't differently if you could go back and do it all over again? How could you make sure to not repeat this mistake again in future?

3. Maintain a positive outlook.

We do not always have control over what happens in our lives, but what we *always* have is control over how we chose to react to it. Someone with a positive outlook is always looking on the bright side of things. Furthermore, optimism is infectious, and people naturally want to be around those who lift their spirits when circumstances seem less than desirable.

Exercise

Think of at least one situation where you tried to accomplish a task, but the outcome did not turn out as well as you expected. What are the good things that came out of the situation? It could be an unexpected blessing in disguise, a lesson learned or a new discovery you were able to make.

4. Know your strengths and how to utilize them.

Everyone is good at something, whether it is a technical or soft skill. Perhaps you are more knowledgeable and experienced in certain subjects than others around you. Knowing how to harness your strengths gives you an edge over others, thus making you a valuable part of a team.

Exercise

What are the technical and soft skills that you have developed over your lifetime? You may have a technical skill, such as drawing, writing, or mathematics. Maybe you are good at keeping things organized, or perhaps you are a natural conversationalist. Make a list of your strengths and think of how they come in handy at work, and in your day-to-day life. Where could you be using your talents more fully?

5. Be willing to admit your weakness and learn from mistakes.

No one is perfect, and the most successful leaders are not afraid of failure – they humbly acknowledge their shortcoming and learn from their mistakes. One of the keys to effective and respectable leadership is the willingness for a leader to communicate their weaknesses, so that others who excel at particular tasks can be appointed to the team.

Exercise

You have listed your strengths, now list your weaknesses. For the weakness that you have listed, what can you do to minimize or improve upon them?

Recall a time where your weaknesses resulted in a less than desirable outcome for an assigned task. If such circumstances were to reoccur, how would you have handled them differently?

6. Learn to show, not tell.

The best leaders are those who walk the talk. You cannot inspire admiration and respect without being able to back up your claims with proactive actions.

Exercise

What value do you believe you bring to the team or company? What would like your team or co-workers to improve upon? How can you work on modeling those qualities yourself, on a daily basis?

Chapter 3

Be a Leader at Work

Your leadership skills are often put to the test when you are tasked with heading a team to complete a project. If you lack experience of being at the helm, the responsibility of being in charge can feel daunting. The experience, however, is a wonderful chance for personal and professional growth. Thus, being given the opportunity to lead should be taken as a test of character. After all, you never know what you are truly capable of until you step up to the challenge.

Follow these leadership guidelines to help you work effectively with your team:

1. Know your team

Everyone, including yourself, have their strengths and weakness. The key is to create a synergy where everyone's strengths and capabilities in a team complement one another in working towards a common goal. By getting to know what each individual can bring to the table, you can effectively make plans and delegate tasks.

2. Have a clear vision.

As the one in charge, your job is to create a clear path for your team to follow in order to achieve your joint goals. Before you can get everyone on board, you must have clarity and purpose in what you strive towards. Once you have clearly established your target or goals, take time to share it with everyone involved. Explain to them the whys and hows of your vision, how it will benefit them in return, and make sure everyone is on the same page.

3. Set realistic targets.

Having a vision – a clear idea of the destination you are heading for – is only half the equation to actually getting there. The next step is to map out your journey. Set **specific** deadlines and milestones that are realistic for everyone involved in the team. Then, formulate an action plan to reach your targets that everyone is able to commit to. Having a solid roadmap towards a goal gives the team direction, and assures everyone that they are under the guidance of a competent leader.

4. Get everyone involved from the beginning.

The most effective way to get everyone to share in the same vision is to have the whole team involved from day one. Rather than setting instructions for them to follow, have the team work together with you on the planning process, before moving into execution. Hold meetings where everyone is invited to contribute their opinions, ideas and suggestions. Encourage open communication and ask for honest feedback regarding your ideas. Most importantly, be open to change. Being open to feedback shows that you value each team member, and that you are willing to accept constructive criticism.

5. Communicate and listen.

Part of being an effective leader is to be a good communicator and listener. Firstly, you need to be able to clearly communicate your visions, goals, expectations, intentions and strengths to others. Next, you need to listen to what others in your team have to say. Nothing makes people feel more valued, and in turn, motivated to do their best than when they are being heard. Communication skills also include the ability to understand what is nonverbally communicated, so that you can create a harmonious working environment and cooperative team dynamic.

6. Be respectful and treat everyone as an equal.

Respect begets respect. Nobody can stand for being demoralized, talked down to and made to feel like their needs do not matter. As a leader, foster a respectful attitude within the team, especially in your daily interactions. Above all, make it clear that everyone on the team is an equal player, and should be shown respect regardless of age or any other factor.

7. Keep communications constructive.

Calm and constructive communication is the hallmark of a good leader. It makes you more approachable, and creates an accommodating environment where everyone feels comfortable expressing their opinions. Be wary of making patronizing, derogatory and negative remarks, and ensure such modes of communication do not go unchecked among other members of the team.

8. Give credit where it is due.

A leader would be nothing without their followers. So, take time to acknowledge effort and celebrate successful milestones as a team. Give praise for a job well-done, and you will be amazed what your team can accomplish. A happy team is a productive team!

9. Be transparent.

Transparency means letting everyone in on everything. This practice can minimize office politics, tension within the team, and underhand dealings. Transparency must start with the leader implementing and maintaining a policy of openness and honesty between everyone involved. That means no one is exempted from certain rules or favored for privileges behind the back of others.

10. Empower people and encourage creativity.

People become motivated to do their best when they feel valued and appreciated for their contributions.

Many of history's greatest leaders are held in high regard because they recognized and harnessed the potential of their followers. Also, remember that everyone has a hand in the outcome of a project. So, why not let everyone be their own leader by encouraging them to take charge of what they are assigned to do?

Chapter 4

Building the Confidence to Lead

Self-confidence is the cornerstone of leadership. Therefore, developing confidence deserves special attention. Not to be mistaken for assertiveness and arrogance, confidence in a leader inspire feelings of assurance and reliability among followers. People trust a leader whom they can trust to guide them towards success. Fortunately, like many qualities that contribute to effective leadership, confidence in oneself is a learned behavior.

You may have met people who have more self-confidence than others. This is could be due to several factors – their upbringing, personal life situation, social status, physical appearance and previous experiences. However, anyone can take charge of their self-esteem. By paying attention to and improving on a number of aspects of yourself, you can tremendously improve your self-confidence. Here is a six-step confidence booster exercise for you to do that. Do take note though, that building confidence is not something that can be done overnight, nor are there any quick fixes. It is a gradual and on-going process.

1. Practice self-acceptance.

The foundation of self-confidence is feeling comfortable in your own skin, knowing that you have skills, talents and capabilities that can be of value. So, time to stop underestimating yourself and downplaying your abilities. Self-acceptance is the foundation for confidence, and only by coming to terms with who you are – flaws and all – can you have a foundation to improve upon. As you will see in the subsequent steps, all of the exercises will add up to being able to enhance your self-acceptance. For now, just get into the mindset of accepting yourself wholly for who you are, and embrace your uniqueness.

Exercise

In Chapter 2, you listed down your strengths and weaknesses (if you haven't done it yet, do it now!). Acknowledge your weaknesses, but focus on your strengths. Then, affirm to yourself that you have enough of what it takes to be your own leader, and that you are enough.

Create a personal mantra, and use this self-affirmation whenever you need a jolt in self-belief. It can be as simple as telling yourself, "I can do it!" or reminding yourself of what you are actually capable of, "I am a competent computer programmer. I have been doing this job for almost a decade now and I keep getting better at it." What's your mantra?

2. Work on your self-image.

How we feel about ourselves has a lot to do with how we see ourselves. The quickest way for you to change how you see yourself is by improving the most noticeable factor – your physical appearance. There are some aspects of our appearance which we have no control over and can only learn to accept, such as height and facial features.

Thankfully, we can change a lot of the things which make us unhappy about the way we look, without resorting to drastic measures, because most of it has to do with lifestyle choices. It should be kept in mind that making the effort to look better must not be equated with conformity. You are not necessarily trying to fit society's and the media's standards of beauty; just aiming to look your personal best, so that you feel good about yourself when you stand in front of a mirror.

Exercise

Make an honest assessment of your appearance. What are your best features and what are you unhappy about? Then, think of realistic and healthy ways in which you can make changes to your lifestyle, which will in turn lead to your outer appearance and self-image being improved. Be mindful as well of what you can and cannot change.

Formulate an action plan that will benefit your body, mind and spirit. Among the things you can do are:

- Start a new fitness program

- Take up a new sport

- Change your hairstyle

- Change the way you wear your makeup

- Learn to dress better

- Begin a better skincare regime

- Adopt healthier eating habits

- Be more consistent with your grooming habits

- Get to bed a little earlier

3. Learn to be true to yourself.

Living true to yourself means letting your authentic self shine through, even when your beliefs and opinions are at odds with the majority. We are often taught that the entire world is a stage, and everyone is wearing a mask to conceal certain parts of themselves from the world. Hence, it is hardly surprising that living authentically can be an intimidating prospect for many. With practice, however, it can eventually become second nature.

Exercise

To be authentic, there is no way around it but to just get into the habit of being yourself. Speak your mind, even if you think others may disagree. Say what you mean, and not what you think others expect to hear from you. Be honest about your likes and dislikes. Learn to say yes or no when it matters, regardless of what you assume others will think. Don't partake in activities or put yourself in situations that you personally do not enjoy. It may not be the most comfortable thing to do at first, but stay with it.

Someday, you will look back and be thankful to yourself for working up the courage to live truthfully.

4. Be grateful.

We tend to lose our sense of self when we keep looking to others and wish for what they have, neglecting the fact that we have plenty to be thankful for in our lives. When you put yourself in a state of gratitude, you begin to notice and appreciate the many blessings around you. The more gratitude you feel for what you have, the less likely you are to feel the need to compare yourself with others. This in turn gives you a profound sense of self-assurance.

Exercise

Before going to bed each night, list at least three things that happened during the day which you are grateful for – big or small. It could be receiving a random act of kindness from a stranger, having a co-worker help with a minor computer problem, or simply the fact that your day went by smoothly. If you're really struggling to come up with anything to be thankful for, go back to the basics; did you have a meal this evening? Do you have a worm bed to sleep in tonight? Do you have friends and family that care for you? If yes, you have plenty to be grateful for, even though we often take these kinds of things for granted.

5. Gain more knowledge and improve yourself.

Knowledge is power, and the day you stop learning is the day you stop living. Being knowledgeable helps us feel confident, especially when conversing in social situations. Additionally, there are a lot of benefits to be had from adding on to your knowledge bank and continuing to improve whatever skills you have worked hard to master. A more indirect way to continue learning and growing is to be more receptive to the perceptions of others and the information all around you.

Exercise

Devote yourself to learning something new every day by getting into the habit of reading at least one article from a website, blog or publication on a website that interests you. Most importantly, figure out how you can apply what you learn in your daily life.

6. Set small personal goals.

There is no greater confidence booster than the triumphant feeling of having accomplished something by yourself. You can do your morale a favor by setting small goals for your personal and professional development that you can strive to achieve on a daily or weekly basis. Be sure to celebrate your successes by rewarding yourself!

Exercise

This final self-confidence exercise builds on the previous ones. Make a to-do list of the things you want to accomplish and set a milestone, with an accompanying reward for each goal.

For instance, if your goal is to lose some weight and dress better, you can set a target to follow a diet and workout plan consistently for three months. When the target is met, you will reward yourself by shopping for new clothes for your wardrobe. (See Chapter 6 for more suggestions)

Chapter 5

Leadership Traps to Avoid

To err is only human, and being a leader does not make you anymore perfect than others. It is always a good idea to keep yourself in check and make sure you do not make these 10 leadership mistakes. It should also be remembered that as a leader, your success is measured by the success of your team.

1. Egotism: the root cause of a leader's downfall.

Ego is a term in the field of psychology that refers to an individual's self-concept. Hence, when someone is said to have a 'big ego', it means they have an inflated view of themselves. Egotism is the need to encourage, maintain and enhance favorable views of oneself.

When your decisions and actions are motivated by personal interest, rather than the best interest of the team, you are acting out of ego. The egoistical leader seeks self-validation, public recognition and fulfillment of various selfish needs, mostly at the expense of others. When you lead with arrogance, you will eventually lose your effectiveness as a leader, along with the respect of your followers.

2. Not having clearly defined and communicated goals.

How much trust can people place in a leader who does not seem to know where they are heading? It is therefore important that the goals which the team is supposed to be working towards are clearly communicated, leaving no room for confusion.

3. Having overly high expectations.

Compassion and understanding seem to be important leadership traits that are often overlooked. Part of guiding others towards greatness as a leader means forgiving people for their mistakes and allowing them to learn their lesson. Expecting perfection from your followers and leaving no room for second chances will only result in people fearing and resenting, rather than respecting, your leadership.

4. Getting too attached to one way of doing things.

Being inflexible in how you get things done is an ego trip that could hinder your team's productivity and progress. If you find yourself stuck, use it as an opportunity to ask your team to pitch in and formulate a solution together. Asking your team for help does not make you a weak leader; it reflects your humility and makes your team members feel valued.

5. Not playing by the rules you set yourself.

When setting rules and guidelines for the team to follow – especially where ethical conduct is concerned – make sure you are not the exception to your own rules. Otherwise, you are simply not practicing what you preach, and nobody likes working with a hypocrite.

6. Using fear as a motivator.

Refrain from using threats on people under your charge to spur them on. You may think that telling someone they stand to lose their job, or your will report their poor performance to the higher-ups in the company could motivate them to produce their best performance. In actual fact, putting pressure on people to get the job done with scare tactics may just encourage them to act unethically out of desperation. Just take a look at what became of the dictatorship regimes throughout history.

7. Playing the blame game.

When problems arise with regard to productivity, a leader needs to step forth to take responsibility and guide the team to a solution. Pointing fingers at your team will get nothing fixed, but will make people question your competency. After all, it was your planning which led them to where they are, right?

8. Not addressing problems swiftly.

Sweeping dust under the rug does not make for a clean house, just as problems will not disappear on their own by being ignored. Whenever issues arise, whether it is something that hinders productivity or conflict among members of the team, see to it that it is settled and do not allow it to escalate.

9. Scolding and humiliating.

Encourage a respectful working dynamic among team members by correcting wrongs and settling conflict in a civilized manner. Shouting at someone and calling them out publicly is extremely demoralizing.

Remember that negativity is infectious. Seeing someone in the team being berated is enough to lower the morale of everyone who witnesses the event, and it may make the work environment hostile. Not to mention, they will feel that they are walking on eggshells under your leadership, which will gradually grow into resentment.

10. Showing favoritism.

A job well done deserves attention and recognition, but singling out one person from the team as a favorite is sure to create unnecessary politics and conflict. There is nothing wrong with encouraging some healthy competition within the team, just as long as no one loses sight of the ultimate goal. As the person in charge, you can make sure competitiveness among team members does not go overboard by staying neutral and being fair.

11. Provide a solution instead of working on one.

You may think you are doing the team a favor by being a problem solver, believing that it is faster to tell people what to do rather than having them figure it out for themselves. However, by "spoon feeding" your team solutions, you miss the opportunity to help them to learn about problem solving. You could also be missing out on alternative solutions from other team members, some of which may be better than your own.

12. Trying to do it all by yourself.

If you want something done correctly and done quickly, the best way is to do it yourself, right? Wrong! When you try to do it all, you will only end up spreading yourself too thin. Moreover, you are not empowering people when you try to take over tasks that they may have been able to do better than you. Delegate tasks, and trust that the person you put in charge knows how to do their job.

Chapter 6

A Dozen More Ways to Improve Your Leadership

As you should know by now, becoming an effective leader is indeed a character building process. It starts with cultivating the habits conducive to personal success. From there on, you build the confidence to take charge, and lead by example. But that is not all! Being a good leader involves continuous self-improvement, otherwise, the ego will take over, obscuring the qualities that initially gained you respect as a leader.

Hopefully you have been following the exercises in this book closely. Here are some more suggestions – in no particular order – to think about adding on to your to-do list, which will contribute to you improving your leadership skills. Consider incorporating them into your lifestyle.

1. Read biographies of great leaders.

To be a great leader, you have to think and act like one, and what better way to learn than from the best? Biographies will give you insights into a successful individual's principles of leadership, and also their thought process. Do not limit yourself to biographies of business leaders; diversify your reading to include life stories of spiritual leaders, survivors, artists and pioneering minds.

2. Try something new and unfamiliar.

Read the type of books you have never considered in the past. Eat foods which you've never tried. Watch a foreign language movie. Venturing into unfamiliar territories is a good way to train yourself to be unafraid of and open to change. You may just discover something new in the process!

3. Make yourself do something that scares you.

Success lies outside of your comfort zone. So, work up the courage and aim to do something that has always made your knees weak. It need not be too drastic. Are you afraid of public singing? Go to karaoke with some friends. Have a snake phobia? Visit a reptile farm. Afraid of watching horror movies alone? Do it anyway. You will feel a rush of confidence and fearlessness when overcoming something you once thought of as impossible.

4. Do something you have been procrastinating on.

Is there something you should have done long ago, but you keep postponing it? Whether it is a task at work, a chore at home or calling a friend you haven't seen for ages, it is time to get to it. Leaders are doers, not passive thinkers.

5. De-clutter.

Keep your personal and work space organized and free of clutter. You will be amazed at the positive effect it has on your morale and productivity.

6. Volunteer.

Giving your time to a cause you believe in is the best way to take your leadership outside the workplace. Besides helping a great cause, being actively involved in a non-profit organization's activities is an excellent way to get hands-on team-building and leadership experience, especially when you are just entering the workforce. Even better, offer to be in charge of planning activities for the organization. You will be surprised to find a lot of non-profits are welcoming of helping hands and new ideas.

7. Do something minor for your own betterment every day.

You do not pick up a habit overnight, but gradually over time. If you are having trouble picking up a good habit or ditching a bad one, make a point to do something every day that will add up over time. For instance, if you want to change your eating habits, endeavor to substitute a pack of junk food with one serving of salad every day, until it becomes a habit.

8. Take a course for self-interest.

Sign up for a hobby course in something that has always been of interest to you. There are plenty of online and correspondence schools offering short informative courses on a multitude of topics, from child psychology to foreign languages. Starting and committing to something out of self-interest is a testament to your individual discipline, which is another mark of a good leader.

9. Change the way you do something familiar.

There may be things you do every day at work that have become so automated and ingrained that they feel as easy as breathing. Sure, there is comfort in consistency, but without change, you run the risk of stagnation.

Think about how you can switch up some things in your daily routine. Again, it does not have to be a major change, just something to shake things up a little. For example, if you are used to replying to emails in the evening, after your work for the day is done and out of the way, why not try doing that task in the morning? You may just discover more efficient and effective ways of doing things.

10. Read more fiction.

Reading more novels and comics may seem unrelated to honing your leadership skills, but reading more fiction stimulates imagination and allows one to temporarily live through the eyes of another. This in turn can encourage original thinking. In fact, some of the greatest thinkers found inspiration in works of fiction.

A perfect example is Elon Musk, who is known as one of the most innovative inventors and entrepreneurs. Musk has always been vocal about his ambitions for space exploration, an aspiration which stemmed from his love of science fiction novels as a child.

11. Learn to step away.

You cannot empower people and allow them to explore their creativity by constantly breathing down their necks. Let them know that you place trust in their capabilities by taking a back seat after assigning a task.

Learning to let go control and rely on others can be difficult, especially if you are one of those do-it-all types. To ease yourself into the process, pick one or two tasks which you are weak at and make it a point to delegate them to someone else in the team. Communicate your quality expectations, but make it known they are allowed creative freedom to do things their own way. Then, step away and let them go about the task, and only follow up when the designated deadline nears.

12. Nurture your spiritual side.

Being more spiritual can train you to be more patient, tolerant and compassionate towards others – qualities which are necessary to be an effective leader. Maintaining some sort of spiritual practice, like meditation, yoga or contemplative exercises, can also help you adopt a big-picture view of life, cultivate emotional resilience and find inner peace.

Chapter 7

Leadership Quotes - Inspiration from the Masters

"The mediocre teacher tells. The good teacher explains. The superior teacher demonstrates. The great teacher inspires."

—William Arthur Ward

"It's hard to lead a cavalry charge if you think you look
funny on a horse."

—Adlai E. Stevenson II

"Our chief want is someone who will inspire us to be
what we know we could be."

—Ralph Waldo Emerson

"Keep your fears to yourself, but share your courage
with others."

—Robert Louis Stevenson

"You gain strength, courage and confidence by every experience in which you really stop to look fear in the face. You must do the thing you think you cannot do."

—Eleanor Roosevelt

"Example is not the main thing in influencing others. It is the only thing."

—Albert Schweitzer

"Leaders must be close enough to relate to others, but far enough ahead to motivate them."

—John C. Maxwell

"The mark of a great man is one who knows when to set aside the important things in order to accomplish the vital ones."

—Brandon Sanderson

"Leadership is not about titles, positions, or flow charts. It is about one life influencing another."

—John C. Maxwell

"You have to be burning with an idea, or a problem, or a wrong that you want to right. If you're not passionate enough from the start, you'll never stick it out."

—Steve Jobs

"A leader takes people where they would never go on their own."

—Hans Finzel

"You don't lead by pointing and telling people some place to go. You lead by going to that place and making a case."

—Ken Kesey

"A man who wants to lead the orchestra must turn his back on the crowd."

—Max Lucado

"Become the kind of leader that people would follow voluntarily, even if you had no title or position."

—Brian Tracy

"I start with the premise that the function of leadership is to produce more leaders, not more followers."

—Ralph Nader

"Leaders must be close enough to relate to others, but far enough ahead to motivate them."

—John C. Maxwell

"Leadership and learning are indispensable to each other."

—John F. Kennedy

"Leadership cannot just go along to get along. Leadership must meet the moral challenge of the day."

—Jesse Jackson

"Leadership does not always wear the harness of compromise."

—Woodrow Wilson

"Leadership is a potent combination of strategy and character. But if you must be without one, be without the strategy."

—Norman Schwarzkopf

"A leader...is like a shepherd. He stays behind the flock, letting the most nimble go out ahead, whereupon the others follow, not realizing that all along they are being directed from behind."

—Nelson Mandela

"Being responsible sometimes means pissing people off."

—Colin Powell

"Do you know that one of the great problems of our age is that we are governed by people who care more about feelings than they do about thoughts and ideas?"

—Margaret Thatcher

"A leader is a dealer in hope."

—Napoleon

"The best executive is the one who has sense enough to pick good men to do what he wants done, and self-restraint to keep from meddling with them while they do it."

—Theodore Roosevelt

"I don't see myself being special; I just see myself having more responsibilities than the next man. People look to me to do things for them, to have answers."

—Tupac Shakur

"I have three precious things which I hold fast and prize. The first is gentleness; the second is frugality; the third is humility, which keeps me from putting myself before others. Be gentle and you can be bold; be frugal and you can be liberal; avoid putting yourself before others and you can become a leader among men."

—Lao Tzu

"Leadership is the art of getting someone else to do something you want done because he wants to do it."

—Dwight D. Eisenhower

"Victory has a hundred fathers and defeat is an orphan".

—John F. Kennedy

"Management is doing things right; leadership is doing the right things."

—Peter F. Drucker

"You are not here merely to make a living. You are here in order to enable the world to live more amply, with greater vision, with a finer spirit of hope and achievement. You are here to enrich the world, and you impoverish yourself if you forget the errand."

—Woodrow Wilson

"If you would convince a man that he does wrong, do right. But do not care to convince him. Men will believe what they see. Let them see."

—Henry David Thoreau

"I cannot trust a man to control others who cannot control himself."

—Robert E. Lee

"The day the soldiers stop bringing you their problems is the day you stopped leading them. They have either lost confidence that you can help them or concluded that you do not care. Either case is a failure of leadership."

—Colin Powell

"Consensus: The process of abandoning all beliefs, principles, values, and policies in search of something in which no one believes, but to which no one objects; the process of avoiding the very issues that have to be solved, merely because you cannot get agreement on the way ahead. What great cause would have been fought and won under the banner: 'I stand for consensus?'"

—Margaret Thatcher

"A leader takes people where they want to go. A great leader takes people where they don't necessarily want to go, but ought to be."

—Rosalynn Carter

"If you really want the key to success, start by doing the opposite of what everyone else is doing."

—Brad Szollose

"'Give as few orders as possible,' his father had told him once long ago. 'Once you've given orders on a subject, you must always give orders on that subject.'"

—Frank Herbert (from Dune)

"I cannot give you the formula for success, but I can give you the formula for failure, which is: Try to please everybody."

—Herbert Swope

"If one is lucky, a solitary fantasy can totally transform one million realities."

—Maya Angelou

"If you would not be forgotten, as soon as you are dead and rotten, either write things worth reading, or do things worth the writing."

—Benjamin Franklin

"If your actions inspire others to dream more, learn more, do more and become more, you are a leader."

—John Quincy Adams

"There is a difference between being a leader and being a boss. Both are based on authority. A boss demands blind obedience; a leader earns his authority through understanding and trust."

—Klaus Balkenhol

"You get in life what you have the courage to ask for."

—Nancy D. Solomon

"In the end, it is important to remember that we cannot become what we need to be by remaining what we are."

—Max De Pree

"We're here for a reason. I believe a bit of the reason is to throw little torches out to lead people through the dark."

—Whoopi Goldberg

"A leader isn't someone who forces others to make him stronger; a leader is someone willing to give his strength to others so that they may have the strength to stand on their own."

—Beth Revis

"Always remember, Son, the best boss is the one who bosses the least. Whether it's cattle, or horses, or men; the least government is the best government."

—Ralph Moody

"In matters of style, swim with the current; in matters of principle, stand like a rock."

—Thomas Jefferson

"It is absurd that a man should rule others, who cannot rule himself."

—Latin Proverb

"It is better to lead from behind and to put others in front, especially when you celebrate victory when nice things occur. You take the front line when there is danger. Then people will appreciate your leadership."

—Nelson Mandela

"Lead and inspire people. Don't try to manage and manipulate people. Inventories can be managed but people must be lead."

—Ross Perot

"Leaders aren't born, they are made. And they are made just like anything else, through hard work. And that's the price we'll have to pay to achieve that goal, or any goal."

—Vince Lombardi

"The greatest leader is not necessarily the one who does the greatest things. He is the one that gets the people to do the greatest things."

—Ronald Reagan

"Only one man in a thousand is a leader of men--the other 999 follow women."

—Groucho Marx

"Don't waste your energy trying to educate or change opinions; go over, under, through, and opinions will change organically when you're the boss. Or they won't. Who cares? Do your thing, and don't care if they like it."

—Tina Fey

"Power isn't control at all--power is strength, and giving that strength to others. A leader isn't someone who forces others to make him stronger; a leader is someone willing to give his strength to others that they may have the strength to stand on their own."

—Beth Revis

"Don't tell people how to do things, tell them what to do and let them surprise you with their results."

—George Patton

"Leadership is solving problems. The day soldiers stop bringing you their problems is the day you have stopped leading them. They have either lost confidence that you can help or concluded you do not care. Either case is a failure of leadership."

—Colin Powell

"Leadership is the key to 99 percent of all successful efforts."

—Erskine Bowles

"Leadership is unlocking people's potential to become better."

—Bill Bradley

"Management is about arranging and telling. Leadership is about nurturing and enhancing."

—Tom Peters

"Management is efficiency in climbing the ladder of success; leadership determines whether the ladder is leaning against the right wall."

—Stephen Covey

"To do great things is difficult; but to command great things is more difficult."

—Friedrich Nietzsche

"To have long term success as a coach or in any position of leadership, you have to be obsessed in some way."

—Pat Riley

"True leadership lies in guiding others to success. In ensuring that everyone is performing at their best, doing the work they are pledged to do and doing it well."

—Bill Owens

"The art of leadership is saying no, not yes. It is very easy to say yes."

—Tony Blair

"Wisdom equals knowledge plus courage. You have to not only know what to do and when to do it, but you have to also be brave enough to follow through."

—Jarod Kintz

"My responsibility is getting all my players playing for the name on the front of the jersey, not the one on the back."

–Unknown

"A good plan violently executed now is better than a perfect plan executed next week."

–George Patton

"The supreme quality of leadership is integrity."

–Dwight Eisenhower

"You don't lead by hitting people over the head—that's assault, not leadership."

–Dwight Eisenhower

"What you do has far greater impact than what you say."

—Stephen Covey

"A competent leader can get efficient service from poor troops, while on the contrary an incapable leader can demoralize the best of troops."

—John J Pershing

"A good leader is a person who takes a little more than his share of the blame and a little less than his share of the credit."

—John Maxwell

"There are three essentials to leadership: humility, clarity and courage."

—Fuchan Yuan

"I am endlessly fascinated that playing football is considered a training ground for leadership, but raising children isn't."

—Dee Dee Myers

"A cowardly leader is the most dangerous of men."

—Stephen King

"Never give an order that can't be obeyed."

—General Douglas MacArthur

"No man is good enough to govern another man without that other's consent."

—Abraham Lincoln

"We live in a society obsessed with public opinion. But leadership has never been about popularity."

—Marco Rubio

"Whatever you are, be a good one."

—Abraham Lincoln

"To handle yourself, use your head; to handle others,

use your heart."

Eleanor Roosevelt

"Not the cry, but the flight of a wild duck, leads the

flock to fly and follow."

—Chinese Proverb

"One of the tests of leadership is the ability to

recognize a problem before it becomes an emergency."

—Arnold Glasow

"The final test of a leader is that he leaves behind him in other men, the conviction and the will to carry on."

—Walter Lippman

"The greatest leaders mobilize others by coalescing people around a shared vision."

—Ken Blanchard

"The growth and development of people is the highest calling of leadership."

—Harvey Firestone

"In a battle between two ideas, the best one doesn't necessarily win. No, the idea that wins is the one with the most fearless heretic behind it."

—Seth Godin

"I cannot give you a formula for success, but I can give you the formula for failure, which is: try to please everybody."

—Herbert Bayard Swope

"Show me the man you honor and I will know what kind of man you are."

—Thomas John Carlisle

"The challenge of leadership is to be strong but not rude; be kind, but not weak; be bold, but not a bully; be humble, but not timid; be proud, but not arrogant; have humor, but without folly."

—Jim Rohn

"A man always has two reasons for doing anything: a good reason and the real reason."

— J.P. Morgan

"If you want to build a ship, don't drum up the men to gather wood, divide the work, and give orders. Instead, teach them to yearn for the vast and endless sea."

—Antoine de Saint Saint-Exupéry

"Remember, teamwork begins by building trust. And the only way to do that is to overcome our need for invulnerability."

—Patrick Lencioni

"No guts, no story."

—Chris Brady

"Leadership is an action, not a position."

—Donald McGannon

"Surround yourself with great people; delegate
authority; get out of the way"

—Ronald Reagan

"If you spend your life trying to be good at everything,
you will never be great at anything."

—Tom Rath

"Average leaders raise the bar on themselves; good
leaders raise the bar for others; great leaders inspire
others to raise their own bar."

—Orrin Woodward

"Don't blow off another's candle for it won't make yours shine brighter."

—Jaachynma N.E. Agu

"Whenever you see a successful business, someone once made a courageous decision."

—Peter F. Drucker

"When you put together deep knowledge about a subject that intensely matters to you, charisma happens. You gain courage to share your passion, and when you do that, folks follow."

—Jerry Porras

"Anyone can hold the helm when the sea is calm."

—Publilius Syrus

"A great person attracts great people and knows how to hold them together. "

—Johann Wolfgang von Goethe

"My job is not to be easy on people. My job is to take these great people we have and to push them and make them even better."

—Steve Jobs

"People buy into the leader before they buy into the vision."

—John Maxwell

"To have long-term success as a coach or in any position of leadership, you have to be obsessed in some way."

—Pat Riley

"A good leader is a person who takes a little more than his share of the blame and a little less than his share of the credit."

—John Maxwell

"A good plan violently executed now is better than a perfect plan executed next week."

—George Patton

"Earn your leadership every day."

—Michael Jordan

"So much of what we call management consists in making it difficult for people to work."

—Peter Drucker

"The art of leadership is saying no, not saying yes. It is very easy to say yes."

—Tony Blair

"The very essence of leadership is that you have to have a vision. It's got to be a vision you articulate clearly and forcefully on every occasion. You can't blow an uncertain trumpet."

—Reverend Theodore Hesburgh

"The key to successful leadership today is influence, not authority."

—Kenneth Blanchard

"A good general not only sees the way to victory; he also knows when victory is impossible."

—Polybius

"A great leader's courage to fulfill his vision comes from passion, not position."

—John Maxwell

"A leader takes people where they want to go. A great leader takes people where they don't necessarily want to go, but ought to be."

—Rosalynn Carter

"The challenge of leadership is to be strong, but not rude; be kind, but not weak; be bold, but not bully; be thoughtful, but not lazy; be humble, but not timid; be proud, but not arrogant; have humor, but without folly."

—Jim Rohn

"Outstanding leaders go out of their way to boost the self-esteem of their personnel. If people believe in themselves, it's amazing what they can accomplish."

—Sam Walton

"A true leader has the confidence to stand alone, the courage to make tough decisions, and the compassion to listen to the needs of others. He does not set out to be a leader, but becomes one by the equality of his actions and the integrity of his intent."

—Douglas MacArthur

"A ruler should be slow to punish and swift to reward."

—Ovid

"No man will make a great leader who wants to do it all himself, or to get all the credit for doing it."

—Andrew Carnegie

"As we look ahead into the next century, leaders will

be those who empower others."

—Bill Gates

"All of the great leaders have had one characteristic in

common: it was the willingness to confront

unequivocally the major anxiety of their people in

their time. This, and not much else, is the essence of

leadership."

—John Kenneth Galbraith

"Do what you feel in your heart to be right—for you'll

be criticized anyway."

—Eleanor Roosevelt

"Don't necessarily avoid sharp edges. Occasionally they are necessary to leadership."

—Donald Rumsfeld

"Education is the mother of leadership."

—Wendell Willkie

"Leadership is the art of getting someone else to do something you want done because he wants to do it."

—General Dwight Eisenhower

"The leader has to be practical and a realist yet must talk the language of the visionary and the idealist."

—Eric Hoffer

"Leaders think and talk about the solutions. Followers think and talk about the problems."

—Brian Tracy

"A man who wants to lead the orchestra must turn his back on the crowd."

—Max Lucado

"Never tell people how to do things. Tell them what to do and they will surprise you with their ingenuity."

—General George Patton

"Effective leadership is putting first things first. Effective management is discipline, carrying it out."

—Stephen Covey

"Great leaders are almost always great simplifiers, who can cut through argument, debate, and doubt to offer a solution everybody can understand."

—General Colin Powell

"Great leaders are not defined by the absence of weakness, but rather by the presence of clear strengths."

—John Zenger

"He who has great power should use it lightly."

—Seneca

"He who has learned how to obey will know how to command."

—Solon

"I am reminded how hollow the label of leadership sometimes is and how heroic followership can be."

—Warren Bennis

"A leader is best when people barely know he exists, when his work is done, his aim fulfilled, they will say: we did it ourselves."

—Lao Tzu

"Where there is no vision, the people perish."

—Proverbs 29:18

"I must follow the people. Am I not their leader?"

—Benjamin Disraeli

"You manage things; you lead people."

—Rear Admiral Grace Murray Hopper

"The first responsibility of a leader is to define reality. The last is to say thank you. In between, the leader is a servant."

—Max DePree

"Leadership is the capacity to translate vision into reality."

—Warren Bennis

"Lead me, follow me, or get out of my way."

— General George Patton

"Before you are a leader, success is all about growing yourself. When you become a leader, success is all about growing others."

—Jack Welch

"A leader is a dealer in hope."

—Napoleon Bonaparte

"The nation will find it very hard to look up to the leaders who are keeping their ears to the ground."

—Sir Winston Churchill

"The most dangerous leadership myth is that leaders are born-that there is a genetic factor to leadership. That's nonsense; in fact, the opposite is true. Leaders are made rather than born."

—Warren Bennis

"To command is to serve, nothing more and nothing less."

—Andre Malraux

"He who has never learned to obey cannot be a good commander."

—Aristotle

"Become the kind of leader that people would follow voluntarily; even if you had no title or position."

—Brian Tracy

"You don't need a title to be a leader."

—Multiple Attributions

"A leader is one who knows the way, goes the way, and shows the way."

—John Maxwell

"My own definition of leadership is this: The capacity and the will to rally men and women to a common purpose and the character which inspires confidence."

—General Montgomery

"Leadership is lifting a person's vision to high sights, the raising of a person's performance to a higher standard, the building of a personality beyond its normal limitations."

—Peter Drucker

"Never doubt that a small group of thoughtful, concerned citizens can change world. Indeed it is the only thing that ever has."

—Margaret Mead

"I start with the premise that the function of leadership is to produce more leaders, not more followers."

—Ralph Nader

"Effective leadership is not about making speeches or being liked; leadership is defined by results not attributes."

—Peter Drucker

"Anyone can hold the helm when the sea is calm."

—Publilius Syrus

"A great person attracts great people and knows how to hold them together."

—Johann Wolfgang Von Goethe

"The best executive is the one who has sense enough to pick good men to do what he wants done, and self-restraint enough to keep from meddling with them while they do it."

—Theodore Roosevelt

"Leadership is influence."

—John C. Maxwell

"You don't lead by pointing and telling people some place to go. You lead by going to that place and making a case."

—Ken Kesey

"When I give a minister an order, I leave it to him to find the means to carry it out."

—Napoleon Bonaparte

"Men make history and not the other way around. In periods where there is no leadership, society stands still. Progress occurs when courageous, skillful leaders seize the opportunity to change things for the better."

—Harry S. Truman

"People buy into the leader before they buy into the vision."

—John Maxwell

"A good leader leads the people from above them. A great leader leads the people from within them."

—M.D. Arnold

"The ultimate measure of a man is not where he stands in moments of comfort, but where he stands at times of challenge and controversy."

—Martin Luther King, Jr.

"The very essence of leadership is that you have to have vision. You can't blow an uncertain trumpet."

—Father Theodore M. Hesburgh

"It is absolutely necessary...for me to have persons that can think for me, as well as execute orders."

—George Washington

"When eagles are silent, parrots begin to chatter."

—Winston Churchill

<u>Conclusion</u>

As you have no doubt seen, there are many factors involved in regard to becoming a successful leader. However, by following the guidelines outlined in this book, you will be well on your way to interviewing well and one step closer to becoming a person of influence who is able to confidently and effectively lead others.

Good luck!

A message from the author,

Steve Gold

To show my appreciation for your support, Id like to

offer you a couple of exclusive free gifts:

FREE BONUS NUMBER!

As a free bonus, I've included a preview of one

of my other best-selling books directly after

this section. Enjoy!

ALSO...

Be sure to check out my other books. Scroll to the back of this book for a list of other books written by me, along with download links.

Finally, if you enjoyed this book, **please** take the time to post a review on Amazon. It will only take a couple of minutes and I'd be extremely grateful for your support.

Thank you again for your support.

Steve Gold

FREE BONUS!: Preview Of

"Interview - How To Best Prepare For An Interview And Land Your Dream Job In 2016!"!

If you enjoyed this book, I have a little bonus for you; a preview of one of my other books ""Interview - How To Best Prepare For An Interview And Land Your Dream Job In 2016!"". In this book, we'll take a closer look at exactly what employers are looking for from interviewees, and how best to prepare for an interview so as to give yourself the best chance of landing your dream job!

<u>Introduction</u>

It is not too much of an exaggeration to think of a job interview as one of the most nerve wrecking situations one can be in. For young job seekers just starting off, it can be a defining moment which – whatever the outcome may be – can have a massive impact on one's self-esteem. For career changers, there's no telling what to expect in the unpredictable job market.

Times have certainly changed, and so have the requirements and expectations of employers; what was acceptable or applicable a few years ago may not be so in the modern age. This also means that hiring practices are no longer the same. Ultimately, when it comes to nailing a job interview, knowledge is power and preparation is key – that will never change. The question then becomes how can one adapt to changing hiring practices and ace a job interview in the current climate? What are the things one should know and how can one be best prepared?

In the following chapters, you will gain a better understanding of the job interview process as well as common interviewing practices that are unique to this particular period in time. You will then be guided on how to best prepare when called for a job interview, from what questions to anticipate and how to best handle the tricky ones in order to give yourself the best possible chance of landing the job. Insights will also begin on making a good first impression the moment you meet the hiring manager.

Getting called for an interview is a golden opportunity afforded only to a handful of hopefuls who apply for a job opening, so you need to make the most out of it.

Good luck!

Chapter 1

The Job Interview Demystified

After sending out numerous job applications and patiently waiting, you've finally got the much anticipated call to go for an interview with a potential employer. Having managed to get a job interview means you have surpassed countless other applicants vying for the job, and are among the shortlisted candidates deemed qualified to fill the position. You are being given the chance to convince a potential employer firsthand that you are the person their organization needs. As such, you want to be sure to make the most out of this golden opportunity by putting your best foot forward and, hopefully, secure the job you want.

Job Interviews: Then vs. Now

In the not-so-distant past, people were oftentimes introduced to job openings through being referred by someone or by browsing the classified advertisements in newspapers. Competition was not as though, and if you were lucky enough to be referred by someone the employer knew and trusted, you were likely to already have an advantage over the other candidates.

However, when the internet became the main outlet for recruitment and job searching in the new millennium, it changed the game. Job applicants began to have easier access to information on who was hiring, leading to a significantly higher responses to job postings. Recruiters were then faced with the overwhelming task of sorting through hundreds, maybe even thousands, of applications and narrowing down potential candidates to a small handful. The selected few would then have to go through a tough interview process until the suitable candidate was found from among the hopefuls.

It is hardly a surprise that recruiters have changed their interviewing practices, and now take a tougher approach when screening for suitable candidates. Thus, job seekers now have additional criteria to fulfill in addition to simply stating their credentials, if they want to land that dream job in todays increasingly competitive environment.

What a Recruiter Wants

A job interview is a twofold process. On one hand, a potential employer will be gauging whether you have the capacity to competently fulfill the required role. The interview also allows for a company to form a well-rounded impression of whether a candidate has the personality and motivation to succeed in the particular industry for which they are interviewing. On the other hand, an interviewee has the opportunity to assess whether joining the organization is in line with their career goals, and is also given the chance to convince the hiring manager as to why they are the right fit for a job opening.

Perhaps the most baffling aspect of job hunting is figuring out exactly what recruiters are looking for. More importantly though, how can one get ahead of the pack to become that one outstanding candidate from many who actually lands the job?

The profile of an ideal employee differs from employer to employer. However, the basic tenets of having integrity, the drive to excel and the ability to learn quickly will generally get one noticed, especially if one has ambitions of climbing the corporate ladder. Even though there is no doubt that hard work, perseverance and diligence are essential qualities for success in any job, there are qualities outside of credentials and experience that will get the attention of employers – namely, attitude and mindset.

Businesses are facing various intense challenges in the current economy and market place. This increased competition has meant that companies now need to be lean and efficient. Thus, oftentimes they need employees who can do more than simply perform one particular function in the company. Favorable candidates are the ones who demonstrate creativity, commitment and passion to the job, showing that they are adaptable in a fast-paced working environment and are able to contribute to the business growth agenda in the industry for the long-run.

In summation, as a job seeker, your career survival and progression depends on how much you can contribute to an organization besides what is already specifically requested in the job description. The job interview is a window of opportunity in which you should be aiming to convince a potential employer that, not only can you fulfill the job requirements, but you can bring more to the table than what is being requested.

Check out the rest of "Interview - How To Best Prepare For An Interview And Land Your Dream Job!" on Amazon.

Check Out My Other Books!

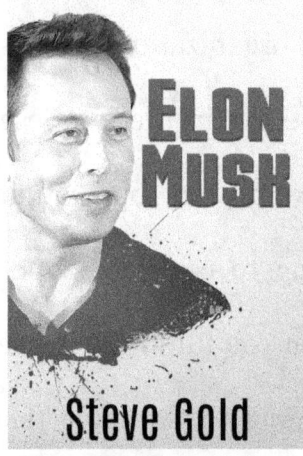

Elon Musk - The Biography Of A Modern Day Renaissance Man

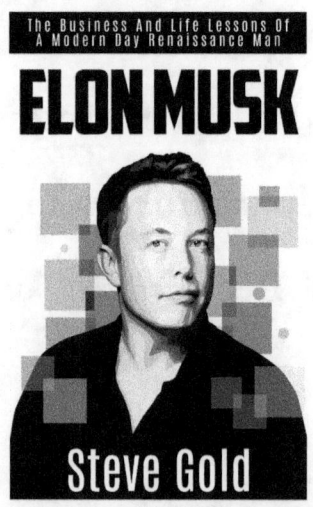

Elon Musk - The Business & Life Lessons Of A Modern Day Renaissance Man

Warren Buffett - The Business And Life Lessons Of An Investment Genius, Magnate And Philanthropist

Steve Jobs - The Biography & Lessons Of The Mastermind Behind Apple

Management - Achieve Management Excellence & World Class Leadership Skills In 7 Simple Steps

Sales - Easily Sell Anything To Anyone & Achieve Sales Excellence In 7 Simple Steps

Arduino - Getting Started With Arduino: The
Ultimate Beginner's Guide

*(If the links do not work, for whatever reason, you
can simply search for these titles on the Amazon to
find them. All books available as ebooks or printed
books)*